AF270652

Dealing with
Disorders and Disease

Autism

CHERITON
CHILDREN'S BOOKS

Published in 2025 by **Cheriton Children's Books**
1 Bank Drive West, Shrewsbury, Shropshire, SY3 9DJ

First Edition

Author: Sarah Eason
Designer: Paul Myerscough
Editor: Jennifer Sanderson
Proofreader: Ellie James

Picture credits: Cover illustration by Doodle Press. Inside: p4: Shutterstock/Fizkes, p6: AdobeStock/Motortion, p7: Shutterstock/Fresnel, p8b: Shutterstock/Whale Design, p8t: AdobeStock/MNStudio, p9: Wikimedia Commons/Orren Jack Turner, p10: Shutterstock/Monkey Business Images, p11: Shutterstock/Stockfour, p13: Shutterstock/1st Footage, p15: AdobeStock/Fizkes, p16: AdobeStock/Halfpoint, p17: Shutterstock/Sciencepics, p18: AdobeStock/Cultura Creative, p19: Shutterstock/Billion Photos, p20: Shutterstock/Imtmphoto, p21: Shutterstock/Monkey Business Images, p22: Shutterstock/Monkey Business Images, p25: Shutterstock/Billion Photos, p27: Shutterstock/Dean Drobot, p29: Shutterstock/Sylv1rob1, p30: Shutterstock/Fizkes, p31: Shutterstock/Sirtravelalot, p32: Shutterstock/Billion Photos, p33: Shutterstock/LuchschenF, p34: Shutterstock/Yurchanka Siarhei, p35: Shutterstock/Gorodenkoff, p36b: Shutterstock/Miridda, p36t: Shutterstock/Chinnapong, p39: Shutterstock/Ben Bryant, p40: Shutterstock/VH Studio, p41: Shutterstock/Peakstock, p42: Shutterstock/Ken Fauzy, p43: Shutterstock/Cheryl Casey, p44: AdobeStock/rtranq, p45: AdobeStock/Rkris, p46: Shutterstock/Alina Kruk, p47: Shutterstock/BearFotos, p49: Shutterstock/StunningArt, p51: Shutterstock/LightField Studios, p53: AdobeStock/Lumos Sp, p54: Shutterstock/Photo Smoothies, p55: Shutterstock/15Studio, p56: Shutterstock/SeventyFour, p59b: Shutterstock/Carballo, p59t: Shutterstock/Tetxu.

Disclaimer: The photographs shown in this book are intended to support the factual content. The publisher notes that the individuals shown in the photographs do not necessarily have the condition/s described in the book.

Printed in China

Please visit our website,
www.cheritonchildrensbooks.com
to see more of our high-quality books.

Contents

Understanding Autism

At a party, people might need to move closer to hear someone they are talking to. They cannot hear over the background noises of music, talking, eating, and laughter. These experiences are quite usual and not extreme. However, for some people, the noises of such a party are overwhelming. They hear everything at the same volume, whether that is someone laughing or shouting or someone sipping a drink. And when someone looks at them, they may experience that as a physical sensation—as if their skin is being touched. These are the experiences of someone with autism.

What Is Autism?

Autism is a neurodevelopmental disorder. This means it is an impairment of the development and growth of the brain and nervous system. As a result, people with autism process information differently from most people. They also experience the world and people around them differently. Everyone with autism has some form of sensory struggle with sight, sound, smell, taste, or touch. For people with autism, their senses can be more intense or more painful or more frightening than they are for most people. People with autism often struggle to interact with others in regular ways. They may also behave, communicate, and learn in different ways from most people.

Made up of Different Shades

A spectrum is a range of different colors, as you might see in a rainbow. Together, the individual colors make up white light. We can think of all the people with autism as having slightly different shades of the disorder. Each has an individual set of symptoms and differences. That is why autism is more properly known as autism spectrum disorder (ASD). However, the condition is more commonly known as autism, and we will refer to it by that name throughout this book.

You probably know someone with autism because it is relatively common. About 1 percent of the global population has the condition—that is more than 75 million people. In the United States, 1 in 68 children has been identified with autism. That is equal to one person with autism for every two classrooms of students in a school. In this book, we will look at what causes autism, how it can be treated, and what it is like to live with this condition.

Autism affects people of all ages. As people get older, they may learn to manage their condition better, but for younger people, finding tools to deal with the disorder and the difficulties it brings can take time.

Autism in Early Life

Autism is a lifelong disorder, and its signs can start at as early as one or two years of age. This is a time when children rapidly acquire and use language, learn boundaries, and figure out how to behave in groups. Many children with autism take longer to start talking. They also have a very hard time learning to take turns and share. They avoid pretend play and cannot understand teasing. They may do things to stimulate their senses, such as flapping their arms, rocking to and fro, or spinning around. All these things can make other children avoid children with autism, because they do not understand the behavior.

The Signs of Autism

People with autism can range from being nonverbal (nonspeaking) to verbal (speaking). They can range from gifted in their abilities to severely challenged. They can range from being very sensitive to not very sensitive to touch, smells, sounds, and other sensory stimuli. Some may have normal coordination and motor skills. Others may find it difficult to walk or grasp things. However, there is a set of typical symptoms of the disorder that apply to many people with autism. These are typical no matter where they happen to fall on the spectrum.

People with autism can often feel isolated and misunderstood.

Understanding Autism

People with autism will often:
- Not make eye contact and prefer to be alone
- Have unusual reactions to the way things taste, look, feel, smell, or sound
- Be interested or disinterested in people, but not know how to relate to them
- Appear to not notice when people talk to them, but respond to other sounds
- Find it difficult to express how they feel
- Have trouble understanding other people's feelings or expressions
- Repeat or echo words or phrases said to them, sometimes in place of normal language
- Repeat actions over and over
- Have obsessive interests
- Have trouble expressing their needs using typical words or motions
- Get upset by minor changes in their normal routine

Fidget toys like these can help people with autism to focus and to ease their anxiety.

Somewhere on the Spectrum

All people with autism fall somewhere on the spectrum. Doctors sometimes diagnose individuals with several distinct subtypes of autism, depending on their symptoms. Today, all subtypes are technically included within autism and are not official medical diagnoses. But, in common practice, the terms are often still used. These terms are well understood and create helpful distinctions between groups.

Autism in Children

Autistic disorder, or childhood autism, is the most commonly diagnosed subtype of autism. It is characterized by impaired development that becomes clear before the age of three. This typically includes abnormal social interaction and communication and restricted repetitive behavior.

Childhood disintegrative disorder, or Heller's syndrome, is the rarest and most severe type of autism. This condition is diagnosed when children develop normally until the age of two, then lose many of the skills they had, such as the ability to walk and talk. They also develop abnormalities such as repetitive mannerisms.

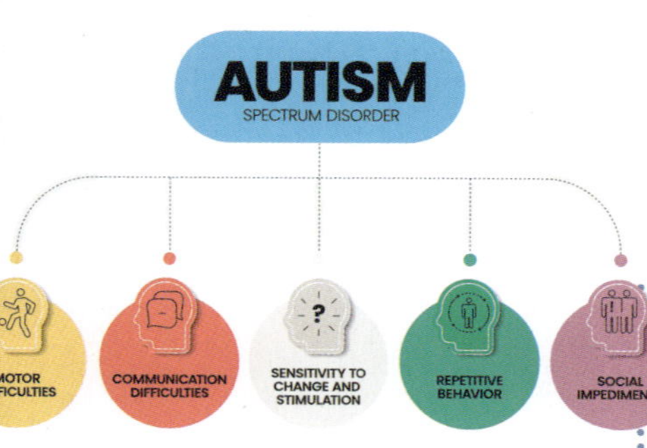

This diagram shows the characteristics often seen in people with autism.

Asperger's Syndrome

Probably the best known subtype of autism is called Asperger's syndrome. People with Asperger's are of average or above average intelligence. They may excel at subjects ranging from art or music to math and computing. In general, people with Asperger's rarely have the learning disabilities that many people with autism have. Children with Asperger's do not have delayed language use. However, like others on the spectrum, they may have difficulties processing language.

Understanding Autism

Children with Asperger's have intense, even obsessive, interests from a young age. These can include interests from animals and cars to reading newspapers and watching old movies. These interests may change over time, or may be lifelong.

Daily Challenges

If you are better at math than your best friend, and they can draw better than you can, we may simply say you have different strengths. When referring to autism, these types of differences are often referred to as being higher or lower functioning. Functioning means dealing with or overcoming the many different challenges of everyday life.

Someone who is higher functioning can speak, read, write, and interact more like people without autism. They can also handle basic life skills such as eating and getting dressed. People who are lower functioning have greater social and behavioral problems. These affect their ability to lead independent lives. These terms are widely used and generally understood. But there is no real definition to describe a person's level of functioning, based on accurate comparisons between different people with autism.

Albert Einstein had Asperger's syndrome. He is famous for being one of the most brilliant scientists to have ever lived.

Education and Autism

Going to school and college can be a difficult experience for children and young people with autism. There are everyday challenges to deal with, for example, students with autism can find it difficult to switch between activities, tasks, and topics throughout the day. The ability to plan and carry out multiple-step projects within set timescales can be difficult, which makes completing homework and studying for and completing tests hard. Students with autism can also find it challenging to deal with change, such as a new teacher, a change in rules at school, or a change in routine such as school outings or event days.

PROBLEMS WITH SENSORY STIMULATION

Because people with autism experience sensory stimulation more strongly than others, this can be a real problem in school and college environments. There, noise from hall bells and buzzers, bright, fluorescent lights, loud voices, different smells, and startling sounds or movements can be very difficult for students with autism to deal with.

Busy educational settings can feel overwhelming for people with autism.

PHYSICAL AND EMOTIONAL

In people with autism, too much sensory stimulation can trigger extreme anxiety and physical symptoms. These include headaches or stomach pain, usually caused by not being able to express anxiety or sensory overload in school or college. Students have to constantly manage their reactions to sensory stimuli, and this can be emotionally draining.

Dealing with Overload

People with autism often use coping mechanisms such as stimming to deal with sensory stimulation. Stimming includes:

Visual stimming: staring at objects, repeatedly blinking, and waving fingers in front of the eyes
Auditory: listening to the same song or noise, repeatedly making sounds, and tapping or snapping fingers
Tactile: rubbing the skin or scratching
Taste and smell: sniffing objects or people, licking, and chewing
Body movements: rocking, swinging, jumping, pacing, running, tiptoeing, and spinning

Stimming often results in a negative reaction from others if they do not understand what is causing the behavior, and interpret it as antisocial rather than a way of dealing with distress.

If people with autism are exposed to too many sensory stimulants, it can make it difficult for them to concentrate.

Dealing with Education

It is vital to respect and value differences in people in all walks of life, and this includes education. Instead of trying to make people with autism behave in a certain way, it is far more helpful if they are allowed to express themselves and learn in a way that best suits them. The problems come when people with autism are pushed into behaving in a certain way. That can lead to the masking of emotions and mental health issues.

EVERYONE IS DIFFERENT

People with autism often say that it helps them and others to recognize that everyone who has autism is unique and their experience of the condition will be different. Some people may find it difficult to focus, while others may become almost obsessed with a topic for a long time. If something is very interesting to them, they may channel all their energy into it.

Adapting teaching to suit an individual's needs can help them learn and find the experience less stressful and more rewarding.

Developing an understanding of their own individual needs and the ways of learning that work for them can make it easier for people with autism to learn.

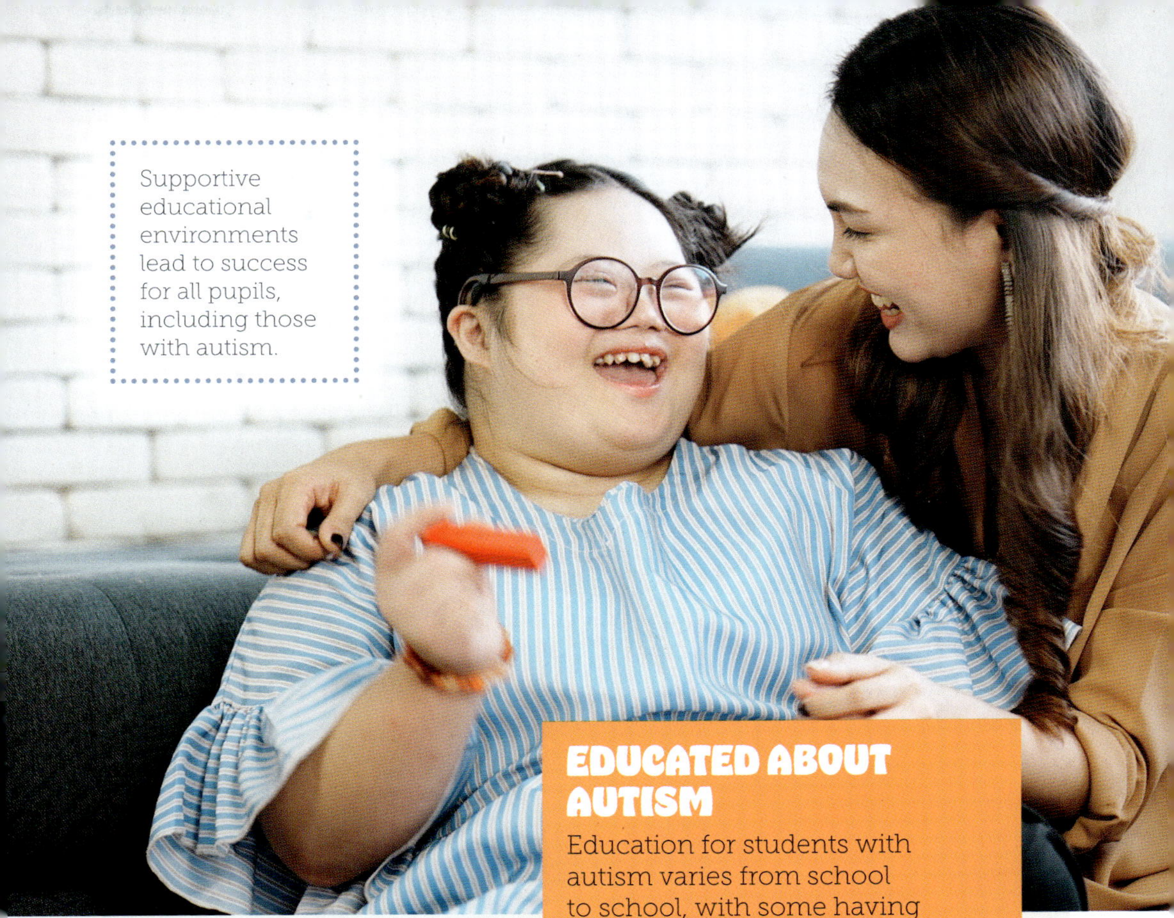

Supportive educational environments lead to success for all pupils, including those with autism.

EDUCATED ABOUT AUTISM

Education for students with autism varies from school to school, with some having teachers who are trained specifically to teach young people with autism while others may be less educated about the condition. A lack of training and education can result in teachers becoming frustrated with pupils who have autism, rather than recognizing their needs. Today, education and training in teaching children with autism is greatly improved in most schools. If teachers are informed about autism and how to help students, their learning experience will be far better —and the teacher's teaching experience will improve too.

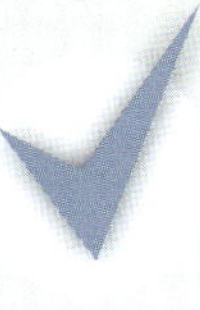

- **A supportive environment helps people with autism learn.**
- **Everyone is unique—respecting differences improves learning environments.**

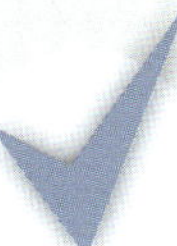

CHAPTER 2

Why Does Autism Happen?

Autism is common globally, yet scientists and doctors are not certain what causes it in different people. However, people with the disorder do have certain differences from the neurotypical population. These differences are evident from a physical examination of the brain.

What Goes on Inside the Brain?

Each person is controlled by their brain. This pink, gray, and wrinkly organ in the skull is the headquarters of the nervous system. The nervous system is a network of nerves that carry information to and from the rest of the body. Messages flow through this vast network to interpret senses, control movement, and countless other things.

Each brain contains about 100 billion nerve cells called neurons. They are not just packed together in a big jumble. Instead, they are organized into different parts with different jobs to do. For example, the cerebellum controls coordination of movement, such as keeping balance. The limbic system is responsible for all the emotions we feel and the things we remember.

In Communication

Different brain parts are in constant communication with one another, and work in a coordinated fashion. This process speeds up from birth. In a child's first few years of life, more than 1 million new connections form between the neurons every second. These create remarkable information highways through the brain, a little like wires in an electrical circuit. Later, the connections are pruned to make brain circuits more efficient and faster. Different neural pathways fine-tune senses such as sight, hearing, and touch, along with motor and language skills, thinking, and memory storage.

"The way autistic brains process information differs from that of neurotypical brains."

Understanding Autism

The brain automatically puts together information to make sense of the world and to navigate it. However, in babies with autism, scientists think that there is a difference in the way brain parts communicate with one another. This makes different pathways develop, leading to different behaviors and responses to the world.

Learning from Research

In 2012, scientists carried out brain scans of people with and without autism. They discovered a surprisingly significant difference in communication between brain parts. The scans showed which parts of the brain become active when people see pictures, read words, or think about things.

In neurotypical brains, there was activity synchronization between the frontal parts and back parts of the brain. The frontal parts process what people see. The back parts process what images mean, and the emotions and memories they produce. In autistic brains, there was a lack of synchronization between these parts.

Trying to cope with a lot of different external stimulants can feel overwhelming for someone with autism.

Finding a calm, quiet space can help people deal with sensory overload if it becomes too much.

Passing Messages

There are significant changes in communication between brain parts in people with autism. These are a result of the way neurons pass messages between each other. Bundles of neurons in nerves carry many messages all the time, to and from different parts of the body. Neurons are special cells with a long part called an axon on one side. They have tufty parts called dendrites on the other side.

Nerve messages move as tiny, very fast bursts of electricity through the axon of one neuron. At the end, they reach a very small gap called a synapse before the start of the dendrites of the next neuron. The messages cross over this synapse in the form of special chemicals called neurotransmitters. When enough chemicals reach the next neuron, the synapse is switched on and the message is passed. Then chemicals called enzymes destroy the neurotransmitters. This clears the synapse in readiness for passing on the next message when it comes.

Nonstop Neurons

In people with autism, studies show that brain neurons have excess amounts of a neurotransmitter called glutamic acid. They also have lower amounts of neurotransmitters that control the amount of message flow, causing the synapses to stay activated for much longer than in people with normal neurotransmitter balance.

"Some people with autism describe their brain as a little like a computer that doesn't have all its updates or latest software."

The Role of Serotonin and Dopamine

Other neurotransmitters show changed amounts in people with autism. For example, these people typically have either too much or too little serotonin. This neurotransmitter regulates learning, memory, sense perception, and many other things. Children with autism often have high dopamine levels, too. This neurotransmitter causes the mind to race and increase sensory perception. This causes an overload on the brain's ability to process information.

Messages are passed from the dendrites of nerve cells and are then captured by the dendrites of other nerve cells.

Understanding Autism

Scientists have also found irregularities in the neurons of people with autism. There are sometimes dendrites that have too many spines or are highly branched. This can result in too many or too few synapses, or synapses that pass messages too strongly or too weakly. Axons can also have an abnormal structure. This leads to the disorganized passage of information through neural pathways between brain parts. These changes in wiring can have a profound effect on the way the brain works in autism.

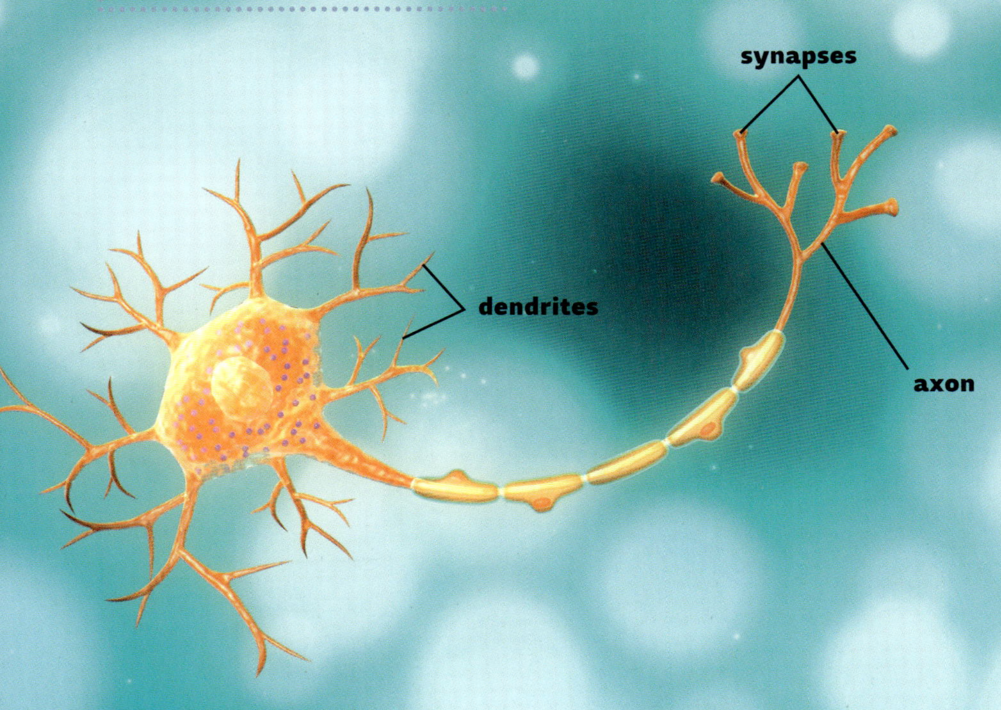

Different Causes

Scientists think that the brain and neural wiring changes associated with autism can be triggered by many different factors. Many of these are genetic, which means that autism can be inherited. Other factors are environmental.

Affected by Environment

When doctors refer to environment, they do not just mean whether someone lives near a park or a forest. They mean other things, such as what chemicals someone was exposed to during their childhood and what happened before or after their birth. For example, one possible trigger for developing autism is being born prematurely (before week 35 of a pregnancy). Another trigger might be being exposed to high levels of certain substances while developing in the womb. These substances include alcohol and narcotics that are ingested by a pregnant woman. Triggers can also include environmental toxins such as pesticides (chemicals to kill bugs on crops). Toxins can also include heavy metals such as mercury, which can be accidentally taken in from the air or water.

Facing Facts

Still other suspected environmental causes for autism include a drug called sodium valproate. It is used to treat epilepsy and bipolar disorder, but recent scientific studies have shown it can harm unborn babies.

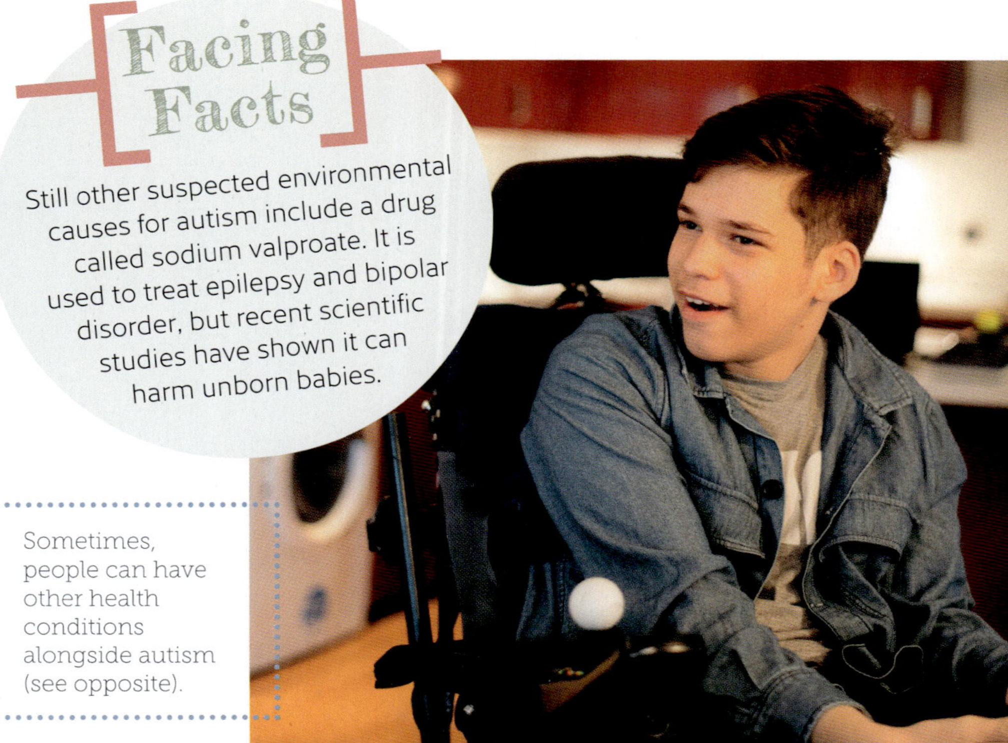

Sometimes, people can have other health conditions alongside autism (see opposite).

Understanding Autism

Several health conditions are known to be associated with the development of autism in individuals. These include cerebral palsy, which is a neurodevelopmental disorder that affects movement and posture. It is the most common physical disability in childhood. Another is muscular dystrophy, a condition that gradually causes muscles to weaken.

Viruses and Inflammation

Certain viral infections such as measles and mumps can also increase the risk of autism in children. Another possible culprit is encephalitis. This is a type of brain inflammation and swelling that is caused by cells of the immune system collecting in the brain and attacking viruses. This illness has an impact on neuron health and the abilities of synapses to transmit messages.

Some parents have blamed the combined MMR (measles, mumps, and rubella) vaccine for their child's autism. However, studies have failed to show any link between childhood vaccines and symptoms of autism.

No Evidence

Eating too much dairy or gluten in one's diet, immunizations, and bad parenting: these have all been suggested as reasons for a child having autism. In looking for evidence to prove or disprove these ideas, scientists have carried out extensive research and studies on patients. Sometimes, it is clear from the data that something is definitely not a cause. This is the case for diet and upbringing. It is also true for the common childhood vaccines that treat dangerous infectious diseases such as polio, chickenpox, and measles, mumps, and rubella.

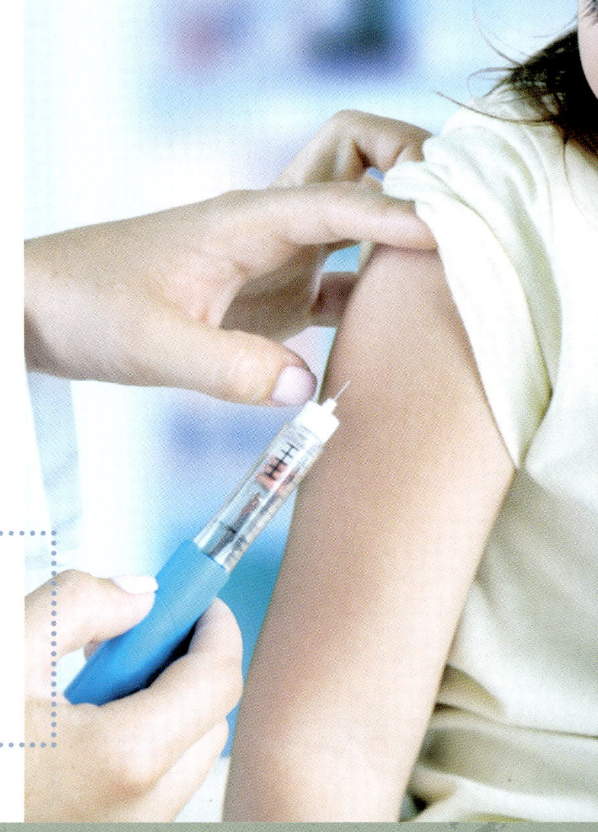

Social Connections and Autism

Social interaction means understanding how people are expected to behave in different social situations, including how they should behave around others. That means paying attention to social information, understanding and interpreting it, and responding to problems. These skills are usually developed during childhood, so that by adulthood people can deal with social situations. However, that is often not the case for people with autism.

DIFFERENT WANTS AND NEEDS

People with autism often have varying skills, needs, and wants during social situations. For some, they may not want to react closely with others around them. They may just want help with meeting needs, such as carrying out a task. Others may want a lot of social interaction, and enjoy a wide range of connections with a lot of different people.

CHALLENGES IN CONNECTIONS

In people with autism, social situations can pose many challenges. They may find it difficult to understand subtle behavior and speech, such as when people use language to hide how they are really feeling, for example, smiling and making a joke about a situation that is actually upsetting and difficult for them. People with autism may also be distracted by things that people without autism would not find distracting, such as a subtle noise in the background, which can make it difficult for them to focus on a conversation. They might also focus on a particular detail, such as a pattern on a person's clothing, which makes it hard for them to concentrate on the conversation.

Some people with autism enjoy social interaction, while others may prefer to spend more time alone.

Dealing with Social Issues

People with autism may find different aspects of connecting with others difficult. These often include:

- Starting and maintaining conversations
- Understanding nonverbal cues, such as body language and facial expressions
- Making and keeping eye contact
- Talking about things that are not interesting to them
- Seeing others' points of view
- Understanding subtle language such as sarcasm and certain jokes

Body contact such as hugging may seem a normal, everyday practice for many teens and their friends, but for someone with autism, it can be very challenging.

FINDING TOUCH DIFFICULT

Some people with autism may find being touched very difficult. Shaking hands, hugging, the touch of a hand on the arm, a kiss on the cheek, a pat on the back—all of these methods of physical contact can be upsetting for people with autism. That can make initial social situations, such as meeting people for the first time, a job interview, or attending a big, noisy event with a lot of people jostling against one another, very hard.

Dealing with Social Connections

Just as people learn academic skills such as reading, math, and writing, they can also learn social skills. They can be learned through watching others behave in social situations, and then modeling their behavior. They can also be learned by just focusing on one social skill at a time, such as smiling and making eye contact, then repeating that skill over and over until it becomes easier to do. These learning methods are often used to help people with autism manage social situations.

LEARNING SOCIAL SKILLS

People who work with children with autism or parents of children with autism find that learning and managing social behavior often works well through role-playing and also modeling the behavior of people without autism. Some methods used are:

- Playing with games that model social situations, such as pretending to go to a party or meet friends at the mall
- Talking about social events beforehand—explaining what might happen and also trying out some social skills, such as ideas about what to talk about or what to do at the event
- Helping children with autism watch how others interact in social situations and encouraging modeling of behavior, such as asking, "Can I join in?" and "Can I sit next to you?"

Social situations can be stressful for people with autism, but they can learn and practice social skills to help them to interact.

LEARNING VISUALLY

Visual supports often help people with autism learn social skills. Using picture cards, photos, stickers, drawings, and videos to explain and learn social behavior are all useful tools. For example, a parent may hold up a picture with different facial expressions, such as a smiling face, an angry face, and a sad face. They might then ask their child to choose the facial expression to use when meeting someone such as a friend at a party.

AUTISM AND THE TEEN YEARS

Many teenagers struggle with social events, not just those on the spectrum. But autism can make this challenging time of life even harder. When people on the spectrum reach the teenage years, there can be even greater pressure to fit in and be part of a group. While parties and social gatherings can help teens with autism learn and practice skills, they can also cause stress and anxiety.

Some people on the spectrum are satisfied with short periods of social interaction, and this should be respected.

Children and teens with autism should never be forced into taking part in too much social interaction if it makes them feel unhappy or uncomfortable.

23

CHAPTER 3

Genetics and Autism

Some people have diseases such as sickle cell anemia or cystic fibrosis. They inherit, or receive from their parents, genes that cause these disorders. The genes prevent cells from functioning properly in ways that lead to specific disease symptoms. In a similar manner, scientists and doctors believe that a person's genes can also influence whether that person has autism.

Looking at Genes

Genes are often described as the blueprint of instructions found inside every cell. Cells are the building blocks of all living things. The instructions inside a cell tell it how to develop, grow, and function. The instructions are not written, but instead are complex structures made up of a substance called DNA. It looks a lot like a ladder twisted into a spiral. Each rung of the ladder is made from a particular sequence of chemicals, like a string of letters completing a word. These "words" tell cells what to do, just as written words in an instruction book give directions for tasks.

Understanding Autism

The gene instructions involved in autism are found in every person. But only some people develop the condition—why? Scientists think genetic and environmental risk factors push the child over a "threshold" and that leads to autism.

"Autism is likely to have multiple genes responsible rather than just a single gene as the cause."

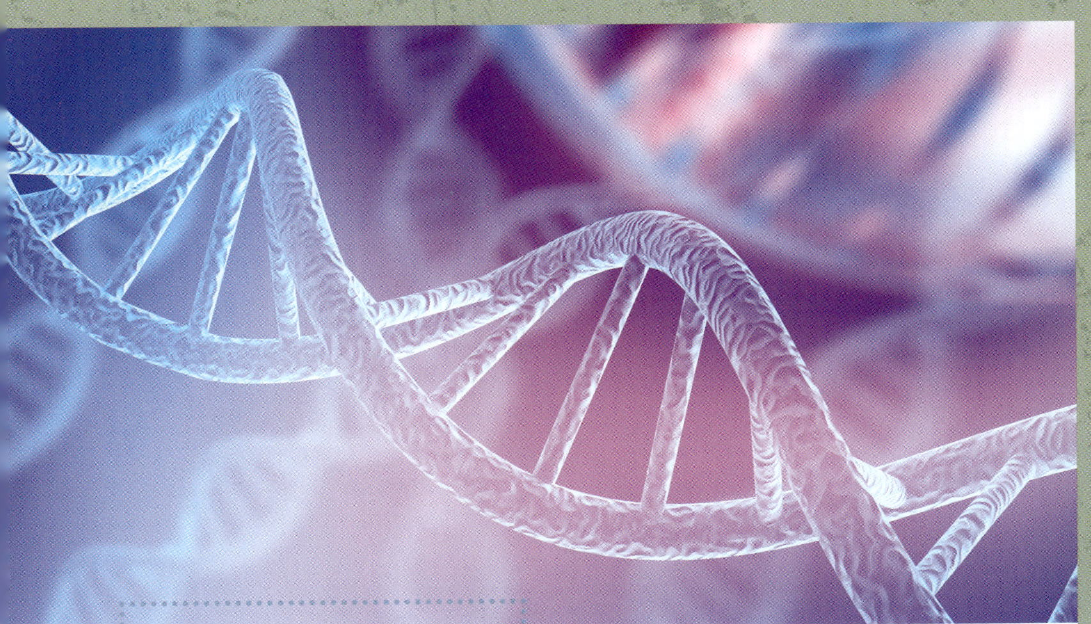

If DNA code is changed as a baby grows and develops, it can lead to autism.

A Blend of Genes

Thousands of genes are twisted and packed tightly into chromosomes inside cells. Each cell in our bodies contains 23 pairs of chromosomes, making 46 altogether. When living things reproduce sexually, one chromosome of each pair from a male joins with another from a female. These produce new pairs in their offspring. Each person inherits from their parents a unique set of chromosomes with its own combination of genes. Whether a person develops a particular condition, such as autism, depends partly on the blend, or combination, of genes they inherit from parents.

Mutated Genes

Can you roll your tongue? If you can, it is because you have one version, or variant, of a gene that controls muscles in the tongue. There are different variants because of mutations in the DNA code. The mutations can happen when DNA is not copied properly as cells divide during growth and reproduction. They can also happen when people expose themselves to harmful chemicals. For example, chemicals in smoke may damage DNA and cause mutations in lung cells. Some mutations are neutral and have no effect. Some mutations are beneficial. Others can cause a disease or condition. Scientists think that mutated genes are responsible for unusual brain development in people with autism.

Neurology and Genes

Scientists studying the genes of people with autism have found that, in more than 80 percent of all cases, there is no identifiable genetic cause. However, the remaining 20 percent of people have autistic symptoms resulting from neurological conditions. These conditions are caused by a mutation in a single gene or chromosome region.

Mutations and Mimicry

Scientists study single-gene disorders using mice in laboratories. They use special techniques to mutate or even remove the normal copy of the gene so the mice mimic the human disorder. They then examine how the genes work in their normal and mutated forms. Scientists have found that genes regulate the complex neural pathways in the brain, such as by changing the quality and quantity of synapses. They have discovered that more than 100 genes are linked to the symptoms of autism, and there may be hundreds more.

Tuberous sclerosis complex (TSC): TSC is caused by a gene mutation on chromosome 9 or 16. This results in benign (noncancerous) tumors in the brain, skin, and internal organs. These can cause anything from skin problems to physical and learning disabilities. Studies report that up to 50 percent of people with TSC show characteristics similar to those of autism. These include poor social interaction, absent or abnormal speech, and repeated behaviors.

Cornelia de Lange syndrome (CdLS): CdLS is linked to abnormalities of three separate chromosomes. Symptoms that would normally indicate autism are found in 50 to 65 percent of people with CdLS. Social anxiety, shyness, repetitive behavior, and refusal to speak except in certain environments or to certain people are common in people with CdLS.

Fragile X syndrome (FXS): This is the most common cause of inherited learning disability. It results from a mutation in a specific gene on the X chromosome. The symptoms of FXS are similar to CdLS. Around one-third of individuals with the syndrome have symptoms typical of autism.

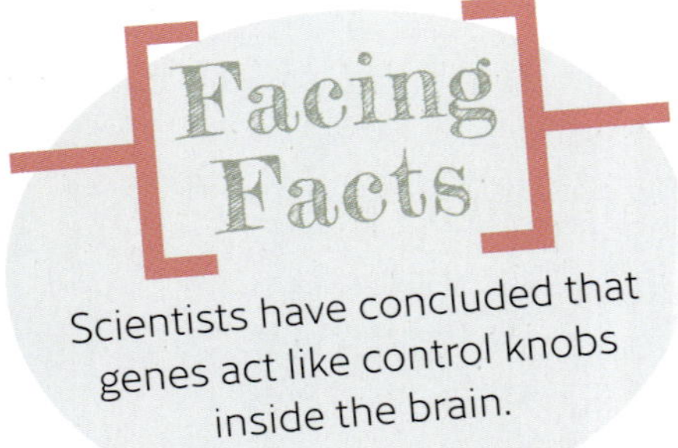

Facing Facts

Scientists have concluded that genes act like control knobs inside the brain.

Understanding Autism

There are other conditions or disorders in which people have fewer symptoms that overlap with autism. They include Angelman, Rett, and Down syndromes. Unlike those with autism, people with Down syndrome are usually skilled at social interaction and have good language skills.

Down syndrome is one of the conditions that can appear alongside autism.

Evidence for Genetics

The study of single-gene disorders provides one strand of evidence to support the idea that genes play a role in autism. So does the study of the spread of autism through the population, which shows clear patterns of inheritance in families.

Caused by Genes

Epidemiologists are scientists who study patterns of illness in populations of people. They look at patterns of illness in families to estimate their heritability. This means the likelihood that their cause is due to genes. For example, one family member has an illness, and there is a higher incidence of that same disease in that family than there is in the general population. That means it is likely that genes play a significant role in the spread of the condition.

More Likely to Develop

There are several patterns that support the theory of heritability in autism. If one sibling has autism, then another sibling has a 4 percent greater risk of developing the disorder than someone without an autistic sibling. For a brother of a male with autism, the risk is around four times what it is for a sister. Epidemiologists have found that males are four times more likely than females to develop autism. This is possibly because males have just one X chromosome, while females have two. So, males may be more sensitive to gene mutations on that chromosome.

Facing Facts

Siblings of someone with autism also have a higher-than-average risk of developing other mental health conditions. These include attention deficit hyperactivity disorder (ADHD).

A family's genes carry information that can shape both the mental and physical development and health of children.

Understanding Autism

Studies of twins are important to epidemiologists. Identical twins share all of their genes, whereas non-identical twins share only half. As a result, identical twins are more likely to share genetically based conditions. Scientists report that if one identical twin has autism, the other twin has around a 90 percent chance of developing the condition. This is nine times the heritability than that reported for non-identical twins.

In the future, gene therapy may reduce the sensory overload experienced by children with autism.

Getting Around Genetics

In the future, people with autism may be able to greatly lessen their symptoms. They may even alter their neurodevelopment by altering the genes that are responsible for the condition. This is possible because scientists have found ways to swap out mutations that cause illnesses. They then replace them with healthy versions. This amazing process is called gene therapy.

Facing Facts

Gene therapy has not yet been used to treat autism, but there are hopes that it will be in the future.

Targeting Genes

Gene therapy targets particular genes in a living thing. Scientists first identify a mutated section of DNA on a gene that is not functioning properly. The gene might be causing a health problem. They then replace the faulty gene with a new, functioning gene. The technique of editing or making changes to genes was first developed in the 1970s. However, it is only in recent times that improved equipment has been available for scientists to use. These include powerful computers and better laboratory techniques for gene editing. Gene therapy has already been successful in treating some illnesses. For example, it has recently begun to be used to treat sickle-cell disease.

Studying Genes

Scientists have so far identified more than 21,000 genes in every human. Each gene is in a different location on one of the 23 chromosomes. Each gene has a different job to do for our bodies. For example, specific genes may cause cells to make particular proteins to build and repair themselves. Or they may regulate the way sets of cells work together. Many gene functions have been discovered. Some conditions involve just one gene function. Others, including autism, are polygenic. This means they involve many genes, and are controlled by their complex and subtle interaction.

Understanding Autism

Scientists think that hundreds of genes are probably involved in autism. They think that people are born with most mutations of these genes, which they carry in nearly every cell. These are called germline mutations. Mutations that occur after birth, affecting a smaller set of the body's cells, are called somatic mutations.

The genes that babies carry determine their appearance and play a huge factor in development from birth through the rest of their lives.

Using Gene Therapy

Gene therapy uses a person's own cells to treat that person. It employs unique cells called stem cells. Unlike most body cells, which do specialized jobs, stem cells are unspecialized at first. But they can turn into specialized cells as needed. They can also divide over and over. Scientists can get stem cells from different places around the body, such as the umbilical cord and the skin.

Understanding Viruses

If you have ever had a cold, then you have been attacked by a virus. Viruses are incredibly small living things, much smaller than bacteria. They have a small amount of DNA in genes protected inside a protein layer. They can only reproduce and increase in number once they get inside other living cells. Once they have infected another cell, they use energy from the host cell to make copies of their genetic material.

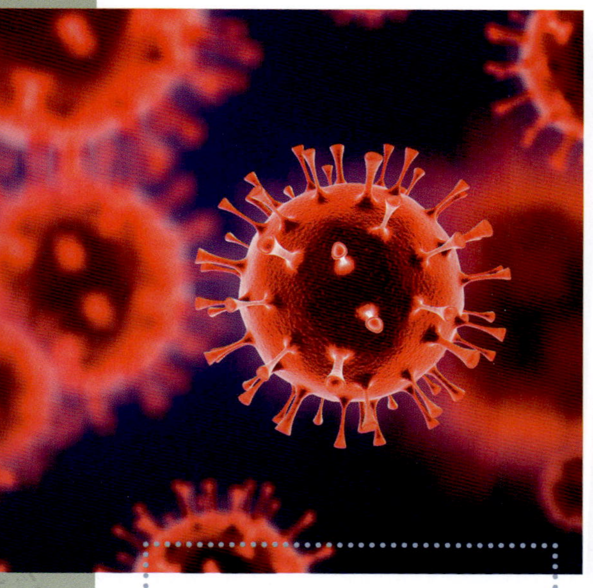

Viruses are normally harmful to humans, but scientists are now using them to help us.

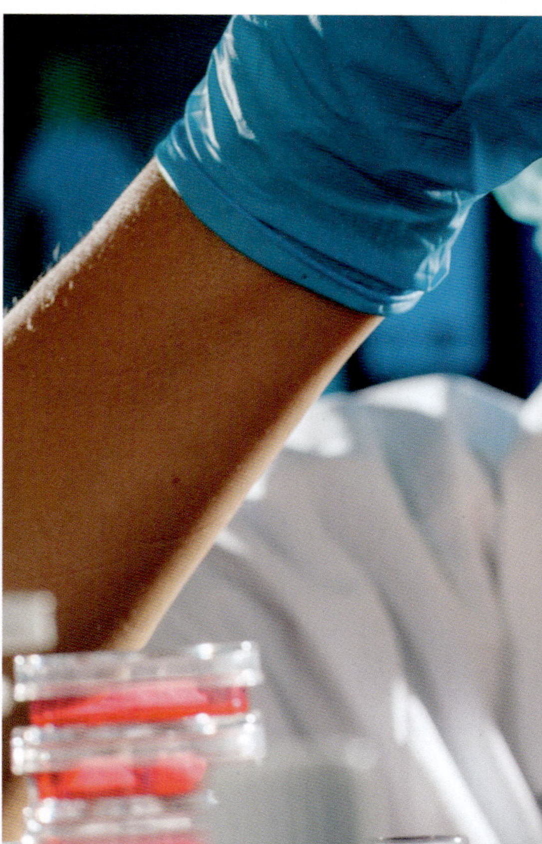

Transporting DNA

Scientists modify viruses and use them to transport DNA. They first remove any of the virus's own genes that cause sicknesses in people. They then replace them with the normal-functioning gene. Scientists inject the stem cells "infected" with the normal gene into the person receiving gene therapy. Once inside the body, the stem cells specialize and the normal copies of the genes start to do their work.

Understanding Autism

In gene therapy for autism, stem cells could form neurons in the brain that make the correct proteins. They may also regulate normal growth and function of dendrites and synapses. This may mend and regrow some neural pathways, increasing communication between brain parts.

Stem cells that carry normal genes are created in laboratories.

Challenges Ahead

Gene therapy for autism is promising. However, it is a more challenging and controversial therapy than antidepressants, for example. The techniques can work well in an artificial laboratory setting. But they are more difficult to predict in the real world—in real patients.

Getting Past the Defenses

The body's defensive shield, the immune system, is populated by a mobile army of white blood cells. These cells defend the body's cells when they detect attack by bacteria or viruses. Some seek out and destroy the viruses. Others create proteins to recognize the attackers to speed up defenses on future attacks. The viruses used in gene therapy can be recognized as intruders, too. The immune system can go into attack mode as the result of gene therapy. If this happens, the body uses up lots of energy and the patient feels exhausted.

Many normal medicines can be injected into the blood. The body circulates the medicine and the blood around the body to where they are useful. But there is a barrier between blood and brain that gene therapy transporters, such as viruses, cannot pass. To get edited cells into the sensitive brain tissue that controls autism, doctors must inject them with a needle. This is potentially harmful because the needle could cause physical damage to the brain. That, in turn, could affect the way a patient experiences moods, thoughts, memories, and other aspects of the brain's function.

While white blood cells are the body's defence against a virus, if overly triggered by therapy such as gene therapy it can lead to an immune attack. This can also cause tissue inflammation and even failure of organs such as the liver. Scientists are working hard to find viruses that are less likely to trigger an immune response.

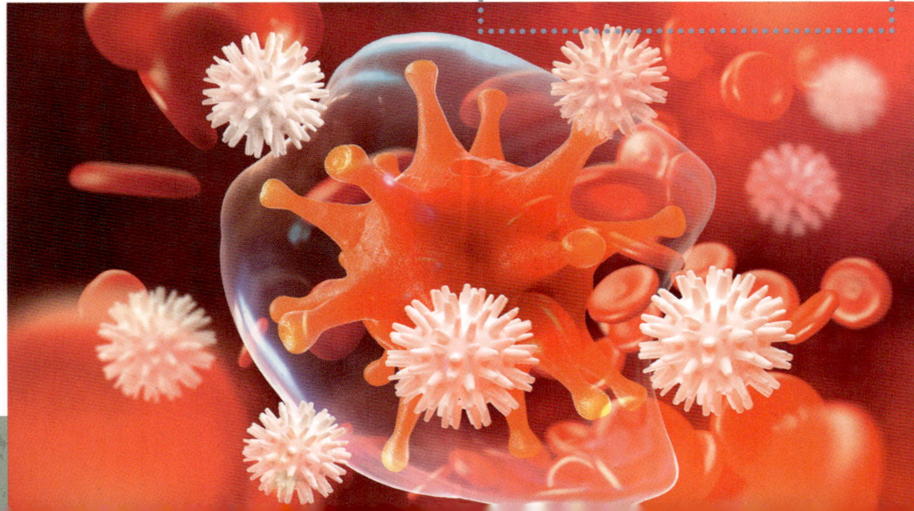

Understanding Autism

Around 1 percent of people with autism lack a working copy of the SHANK3 gene. This gene is critical for brain development and contains instructions for a protein that helps neurons communicate with one another. It also helps organize many other brain proteins in coordinating neuronal responses to incoming nerve messages. Researchers bred mice with autistic symptoms by using laboratory techniques to turn off SHANK3. The symptoms included repetitive behavior such as constant grooming and social avoidance. They then turned the gene back on by giving the mice a special drug. Autism symptoms reversed, even in adult mice. This finding hints that brains in mature mice can at least partially rewire themselves. This work is exciting, but lengthy trials must be carried out to make sure the technique is safe before it can be tested on humans.

Gene therapy tests on mice are showing encouraging results for autism and other conditions.

Great Potential

Gene therapy is highly promising. It has the potential for rapid improvement in symptoms of autism, even rewiring brains. However, at this time, there is uncertainty about what improvements are possible.

A Costly Treatment

Stem cell therapy is increasingly being offered commercially. Centers promise major transformations—at a cost—for people with a variety of conditions. Desperate parents and caregivers of people with autism may be tempted to try anything to help, even if it nearly bankrupts them. However, very few therapies are proven to be effective. In some cases, stem cell treatment for one condition can even lead to autistic symptoms. Also, people must think about the links between cancers and autism. Could tweaking a gene to deal with autism create cancers?

More Research Needed

The way forward is for reputable organizations to carry out more research into the effectiveness of treatments at these centers. The public needs to know what improvements or changes they can realistically expect from such treatments. Currently, there is no quick fix for people with autism.

What Could Change?

Gene therapy is controversial for several reasons. One is that it opens the possibility for misuse. Autism is a condition that is often seen as bad for an individual. It is logical that some people would like to remove from cells the mutated genes that are responsible for the condition. However, who decides what is normal and abnormal in a person's set of genes? Could the use of gene therapy make society less tolerant of people who are different?

[**Facing Facts**]

People are concerned that gene therapy could remove all the diversity in our society, and that would be harmful for everyone.

Understanding Autism

Every person with autism has a different set of symptoms and reactions to various therapies. For this reason, scientists are developing personalized gene therapy to help symptoms. Neurons grown from a patient's own stem cells could be tested in laboratories by turning genes off and on. Then scientists may be able to figure out how genes work together to control what goes on in a person's brain. They can then develop specific therapies. These may include more effective drugs to calm anxiety or to strengthen synapses and electrical communication within a person's brain.

CHAPTER 4

Help with Autism

When a sick patient goes to a clinic, the patient's doctor or other healthcare workers will carry out tests. These include analyzing blood samples to find out what is wrong. Such tests help doctors diagnose anything from heart disease to a bacterial infection. They also help them determine what treatment a patient needs to feel better. However, there are no simple medical tests for diagnosing autism. Screening for autism is a longer and far more involved process.

Checking Development

Developmental screening is a short test to tell if children are learning basic skills by the right age. A doctor will ask the parents questions about what a child has been like since birth. They talk and play with the child during an exam to see how the child speaks, behaves, learns, and moves. A delay in normal development in any of those areas, such as not responding to their name or copying phrases, could be one sign of autism.

Understanding Autism

Autism does not reveal itself the same way. Studies have shown that one-third to one-half of all parents of children with autism noticed a problem before their child's first birthday. Nearly 80 to 90 percent saw problems by 24 months of age. To be able to spot and track developmental changes through time, it is important that parents take their children for screening at regular intervals. Screenings are recommended at 9, 18, and 24 or 30 months of age.

Screening for autism in children is carried out by healthcare professionals who know what to look for.

Careful Reviews

A screening session is brief. Whatever a doctor finds, there is still the possibility that the child was having a bad or unusual day. It may not be representative of the child's actual mental state, abilities, or behaviors. That is why developmental history and input are important in reaching an accurate diagnosis. These can come from family members, caregivers, as well as teachers or workers at schools, colleges, or childcare centers. The process of diagnosis can also rule out other conditions, such as Down syndrome and Tourette syndrome. These conditions could produce similar symptoms to autism.

"The characteristics of autism can be very varied. Two people with the same diagnosis can have different needs and require different support."

A variety of health professionals may work with children and young adults with autism. They specialize in treating the condition.

The First Step

Screening is the first step toward an autism diagnosis. When someone is screened and suspected of having the disorder, they may be given a more thorough diagnostic evaluation. It is important to be certain of such a diagnosis because it has big implications for a patient. Although it can be an initial shock to receive the diagnosis, it can also be useful in the long term and relieve some anxieties. For people with autism and their families, a diagnosis can help explain the difficulties they have had so far in life. It may also enable people to get better access to support that can help them in the future.

Weighing It All Up

A diagnostic evaluation includes a thorough assessment of behavior and development. It also includes a number of tests. For example, people have hearing tests to see how sensitive they are to noises. They can also show whether deafness is preventing them from hearing what others say and responding. They also have eye tests, gene testing to screen for genetic disorders, and other medical tests. The evaluation is often carried out by specialist doctors. These include developmental pediatricians, doctors with special training in child development and children with special needs.

Set Tests to Use

Although autism takes many forms, its diagnosis must be unbiased. That is why specialists use standard tests to assess patients for autism. They use the Diagnostic and Statistical Manual, also called DSM-5. In DSM-5, people are defined as having autism if they satisfy certain criteria. These include having major difficulty in communicating and interacting with people in many situations.

A hearing test is one of the key markers used to help diagnose autism in children.

Experts need to know how severe a patient's autism symptoms are to decide how much support they need. For example, someone with Level 3 autism has very severe problems communicating. They also have such difficulty dealing with change that they will need a great deal of support.

Understanding Autism

The earlier someone is diagnosed with autism, the better. This will give the person more time to learn how to behave and communicate. They can then become far better at dealing with any difficulties they have. They can also make the most of the things they are good at.

A diagnosis can help people better understand the difficult emotions they encounter.

Learning Skills

For people with autism, it can take a lot of effort to behave the way other people expect them to. Learning these skills may require special teachers who are experts in helping people with special needs. These professionals encourage and reward positive behaviors, such as helping others. They ignore or gently discourage negative behaviors, such as shouting out loud. They also know how to maximize a child's abilities. For example, many children with autism have short attention spans. They respond best if tests always happen the same way, following a script. With this information in mind, teachers may break down skills into smaller, easier-to-follow steps.

Help from Therapists

People diagnosed with autism may also have help from occupational therapists. These professionals help people with autism to live as independently as possible. They teach them life skills, such as how to dress and feed themselves. Even bathing can be a challenge for some people with the condition. They may need to overcome difficulties with the feel of water on their skin while bathing. People with autism may need help learning about the dangers of water: water can drown and hot water can scald.

Better Communication

Treatment of autism involves helping people communicate better. Speech therapists teach patients to speak more clearly and build up a better vocabulary. They can teach them to speak in varied tones, stop repeating what people say, listen better, and wait for gaps in a conversation before they speak. People with autism must also learn not to take the meaning of phrases literally. For example, "It's raining cats and dogs" refers to the weather, not to animals falling from the sky!

Not Easy to Treat

People with a headache often take headache pills to get rid of the pain. People with autism do not have such an easy solution. There is no single medication to treat the range of symptoms associated with the condition. There is no treatment that is specific to autism. Different medications can ease particularly serious impacts of autism in some people. But they should be seen as only one part of an important range of therapies. These include psychological, behavioral, and educational programs.

Aggressive and challenging behavior: Tantrums, self-harm, and other negative behaviors may be calmed by taking drugs called antipsychotics. For example, risperidone changes the amount and action of certain neurotransmitters in synapses in the brain. These neurotransmitters include serotonin and dopamine.

Depression: Continuous low mood can be treated with antidepressants. These medications flood the brain with neurotransmitters that improve communication between neurons. They also strengthen information pathways in brain parts controlling mood. Any of these medications, plus medications to treat seizures, sleep problems, and other autistic symptoms, can have side effects.

Facing Facts

Side effects from medication for autism are secondary, usually unwelcome, responses to taking a drug. They may include weight gain, drowsiness, or rashes. To reduce the risk of these side effects, the amount and frequency of autism-related medications needs to be carefully monitored by a doctor. Regular checkups are needed to see how the medication is working.

Music therapy can be very beneficial for children with autism.

Other Methods

Here are just a few of the many other possible therapies that can help people diagnosed with autism.

Talk therapy: Many people with autism can benefit from talk therapy sessions with trained psychologists. These professionals can help people identify unhealthy thoughts and behaviors in themselves and others. They can replace them with healthy, positive ones. The aim of talk therapy is to help people understand how their thoughts, behaviors, and emotions interact with and affect one another.

Sensory interventions: Some people with autism may have highly acute senses that can be helped by specialist interventions. For example, aromatherapy can help people overcome aversion to particular smells. Auditory treatment can help people retrain their ears to block out background noise so they can concentrate on speech.

Music therapy: Singing songs can help people with autism learn and understand language, link words together, and learn when not to make sounds. Making music on a variety of instruments helps with motor skills and nonverbal self-expression, too.

Many children with autism love animal therapy. It is fun and helps soothe senses.

Animal therapy: Horseback riding or working with dogs can all soothe sensory stimulation. They can help some people with autism learn about behavior and communication.

Health and Autism

It important to remember that many people with autism do not see it as a condition, but just a different way of thinking and being rather than something they need to manage. It is also important to note that the health needs of people with autism can differ greatly from one person to another and can change over time, too. Some people with autism can live healthy lives independently, with little or no need for assistance. Other people with autism may have disabilities that mean they need lifelong care and help.

HEALTH ISSUES AND AUTISM

Certain conditions coexist in some people with autism. People with autism may often have epilepsy (see opposite). Some may suffer from depression and anxiety, and ADHD can also be a factor. People with ADHD have trouble with focus, remembering things, managing time and organization, and hyperactive behavior. People with autism may also have other serious health issues such as bipolar disorder, schizophrenia, and Down syndrome. Obsessive compulsive disorder (OCD) may also be seen in people with autism.

ANXIETY, DEPRESSION, AND AUTISM

Anxiety affects almost half of people with autism. The symptoms of anxiety range from difficulties with expressing emotions to physical symptoms, such as a fast or racing heartbeat, aching muscles, and stomach pain. Social anxiety is common, with people with autism having concerns about meeting new people and managing social situations. Rates of depression are much higher in people with autism than in those without the condition. Many people with autism have sleep problems, and self-harming can result because of anxiety and depression.

About 26 percent of adults with autism and 7 percent of children with autism suffer from depression.

FOOD, DIGESTION, AND AUTISM

Issues around food can be seen in many children with autism—in fact, eating problems affect about seven out of 10 children with autism. Issues range from restricting foods because of a dislike of certain tastes and textures to overeating and obesity, because of an inability to sense when the stomach is full. Some children overeat to soothe themselves when they experience anxiety or sensory overload. Children may also eat nonfood items, which is known as pica. This is often seen in children severely affected by autism. Digestive problems are common in people with autism, too.

Epilepsy and Autism

Epilepsy affects up to one-third of people with autism. That is a high number compared to the statistics in people without autism—just 1 to 2 percent of the general population suffer from epilepsy. The condition can be very debilitating, and symptoms include:

- Unexplained staring spells
- Sudden, involuntary movements
- Confusion
- Severe headaches
- Sleepiness or drowsiness
- Broken sleep
- Unexplained changes in emotions or abilities to do things

Some people with autism may have trouble coordinating large muscles, which can make activities such as dancing difficult.

Dealing with Health

The health conditions that often accompany autism are better understood today than they once were. Health professionals now have a wide range of treatments and therapies available for people with autism, to help them manage complex health issues and improve both their physical and mental wellbeing.

MANAGING MENTAL HEALTH

Therapy programs such as cognitive behavioral therapy (CBT) have been adapted especially for people with autism, to help them manage anxiety and depression. The therapy has proven very effective in helping children, teens, and adults with autism. Strategies are also used to help manage ADHD, and in some cases, medication may be used too.

MANAGING FOOD AND SLEEP

Autism clinics usually have specialized feeding programs run by behavioral therapists and nutritionists to help children manage feeding issues such as pica, overeating, and restrictive eating. Likewise, strategies for improving sleep in children and teens are now available, based on research into sleep issues in people who have autism. In particular, trying to limit screen time in the evening and before bed has been shown to improve sleep.

Changes to diet may help improve digestive issues in people with autism, for example, trying to ensure the diet includes plenty of fiber and water.

Getting regular daily exercise can help improve sleep, and reducing stressful activities can be beneficial too.

CBT can help people learn to manage difficult thoughts and emotions.

Food and nutrition are vitally important to both physical and mental health, so practitioners will work with children and parents to help them understand eating problems, what might be causing them, and how to manage them at home.

Living with Autism

There are many day-to-day situations that can be incredibly stressful for someone with autism, from simple tasks such as grocery shopping through using the bus to go to school or work. However, although the challenges of living with autism can be considerable, many people with the condition go on to live independently. Having a supportive and understanding family is often key to being able to maintain independence.

Challenges for Caregivers

For the families of people with autism, life can be very challenging. Parents or main caregivers are responsible for dealing with difficult behaviors, organizing treatments for symptoms, and helping to organize routines for the person with autism. They have the worries of planning for the future. That includes the potential work, study, or independent living of the person. All of this occurs alongside their own regular tasks. This includes preparing meals, and caring for other children and older relatives.

Siblings Too

Siblings of someone with autism can understandably feel overlooked by parents at home. They may feel very embarrassed by their autistic sibling's behavior in public. It can feel unfair if the person with autism is not scolded for what they do, but the neurotypical sibling is.

People with autism go on to have families, work in jobs, and many excel in their careers.

Understanding Autism

Autism affects a whole family. It is important for people to discuss with each other their feelings about it. This can sometimes be easier when families get the help of a trained family therapist. It is also very helpful for families to stay involved in their community. They can participate in everything from fundraising events to walking in the local park, and not shut themselves away. Staying involved allows the person with autism to experience different social settings and relationships. Some families meet up with other families that have members with autism to share experiences with empathetic people.

"While people with autism do face challenges, with the right support in place, they are more than capable of living fulfilling and happy lives."

A Plan for Living with Autism

We are all individuals with quirks, strengths, and weaknesses, so it is no surprise that autism is not a one-size-fits-all condition. People with autism and those who support them need varying strategies. These help them deal with our ever-changing world.

Spell It

One strategy is based around five principles that start with the initial letters S-P-E-L-L.

Structure: People with autism often feel safer, less anxious, and learn best if their lives have structure. Predictable environments and routines help them rely on others less. They also help them to independently go about their lives. Visual aids such as objects, photos, or cartoon strips provide structure.

Positive: Positive approaches and expectations help people with autism build self-confidence and self-esteem. For example, someone may have trouble coping in social situations but they have helpers who have positive expectations. If these helpers really believe the person with autism can succeed in social events, that person will probably make a greater effort. Afterward, the person may feel glad to have participated. They may also be motivated to learn better social skills or ways to make social situations less stressful.

Empathy: It is important for people with autism to try to explain to others how they see the world. Others must also learn how to see the world from the person with autism's standpoint. Empathy allows people to see what motivates or interests people with autism. It helps them understand what preoccupies or frightens them.

Low arousal: People with autism may be unpleasantly affected by particular sensory stimuli. So, it is helpful if they live, study, and work in uncluttered places. Triggers such as noise levels and color schemes should be carefully considered. Also, consider a quieter restaurant with fewer, clear choices of what to order. This may suit a person with autism better than a noisy, busy place with a long, hard-to-understand menu.

Links: Someone with autism may seem trapped inside their own experience. However, they really benefit from strong links with others. A person with autism may prefer working with a regular caregiver or therapist. This is better than seeing a different person each time. People with autism often prefer structured days with fixed sequences of tasks. These can be shown on checklists or large-scale visual calendars.

Understanding Autism

Visual aids help people with autism understand things in ways that written words cannot. They can be about anything from the proper use of toilets to what to expect when going to the movies.

Facing Facts

People with greater difficulties from autism may need continued high levels of support into adulthood. They may leave home and live in sheltered accommodation where resident assistants and other personnel can watch over them. Support workers may help them find job opportunities. They may find work in which the environment or task expectations do not cause excessive anxiety.

People with autism need a trusted, supportive network of family and friends. This allows them to forge strong and important links with others.

Employment and Autism

People with autism often have a huge amount to contribute to the world of work. It's a known fact that some of history's most creative and inventive people were on the spectrum. They include Sir Isaac Newton, Wolfgang Amadeus Mozart, Albert Einstein, and Steve Jobs, to name a few. From amazing contributions to science, music, and technology, all of these famous names made a mark. And they were all able to find an area of work where their unique skills allowed them to shine. However, for many people with autism, finding a job and going to work can be challenging.

PROBLEMS WITH SENSORY STIMULATION

Because people with autism experience sensory stimulation, certain workplace environments can be difficult to deal with. Many people with autism find it hard to work in noisy places, or places in which there are bright, flashing lights. That can make it difficult to work in jobs that might require people to deal with unpredictable and changing environments.

Jobs that involve loud, bright, stimulating workplaces may not suit people with autism.

DEALING WITH OTHER PEOPLE

Taking on jobs that involve a lot of social interaction can also be a challenge. Roles such as working in customer service, managing large teams of people, or teaching may not suit people with autism. However, some people with autism have managed to overcome difficulties and thrive in these roles.

FINDING FOCUS DIFFICULT

Some jobs demand a high level of organization and planning. Many people with autism struggle with time-management skills, organization, prioritizing tasks, and planning. Job roles in which these skills are vital may not suit them and they may find them stressful.

Too Much to Handle

People with autism sometimes talk about "having a meltdown." This refers to feeling overwhelmed and unable to deal with things. During a meltdown, people may:

Cry: this is a natural response to stress and helps release pent-up emotions

Shout, hit things, or pace: getting angry verbally by shouting and physically by hitting objects is another way of letting out emotions when a person feels overwhelmed, as is pacing up and down

Withdraw: people may become very quiet and find it hard to talk to anyone

Not only is it difficult to deal with a meltdown in a workplace, people with autism also have the added pressure of worrying about what coworkers or employers may think of them.

Dealing with Employment

Studies have shown that, when matched with a job that fits their skills, people with autism can be up to 140 percent more productive in the workplace than people without autism! Despite this, it has traditionally been difficult for people with autism to find a role in the workforce, but that is beginning to change.

Today, many people recognize that embracing all aspects of diversity, including neurodiversity, leads to a more well-rounded, balanced, and productive workplace.

A DIVERSE WORKFORCE

Many large organizations are now beginning to see the value of a diverse workforce. For example, some large accounting firms feature neurodiversity programs that invite adults with autism who have exceptional math skills and focus to join—recognizing that these are traits many neurotypical people do not have. Smaller companies too are building a workforce that is more diverse, creating jobs that suit the strengths and abilities of employees with autism.

School counselors and agency personnel are now using special tools and tests to help people with autism discover what careers might suit them so they can pursue career paths that work for them. People with autism who have found a path into the workplace, and the career advisors who work with people with autism, often talk about "job carving." This means identifying your strengths and skills, understanding challenges that you find especially difficult, and then finding a role that best suits you with all those factors in mind.

Respect and Support

Despite positive changes in the workplace, it's still a fact that most adults with autism are underemployed. Many have only part-time jobs or are doing work that they feel does not match their skills. That needs to change.

Adjusting work environments to help meet the needs of neurodiverse people will make it possible for more people with autism to enter the workplace—and that means a more diverse and productive workforce.

We need to recognize and change barriers in the workplace for people with autism. It can be difficult for some people with autism to manage the stimuli in many workplaces, which are not adapted to cater for them. Social anxiety and other issues around interaction and communication can also prevent people with autism from entering the workforce.

People have the right to decide whether to tell their employer about their autism, or to keep it to themselves. They should choose to do whatever feels right for them at the time.

Autism and the Future

Today, autism is on the rise and people are not really sure why. Part of the reason might be better screening. But part may be some as-yet-unknown combination of genetic and environmental influences. The wider public is becoming aware that autism is the result of physical differences in brain wiring. It is a health condition as real as cancer, not a sign of weakness or poor behavior. However, society needs to develop a better understanding of people with autism.

On the Horizon

Effectiveness of therapies is being improved by earlier screening. For example, some new types of brain scans can spot brain disconnects in children as young as six months of age. And new therapies are emerging all the time to treat autism symptoms. These are helped by projects for screening mutated genes and determining their functions and interactions in more families with autism.

The Biggest Screening Project

The Autism Speaks MSSNG Project is the world's largest genetic screening program for autism. Its name represents the missing information about autism that scientists are seeking.

So far, they have analyzed genes in more than 11,000 people affected by autism. They found 61 gene variations in common—most controlling the production of proteins and other chemicals in brains. Researchers say that some of the same gene variants may be found in people with autism at different ends of the spectrum. Some individuals who carry the mutations do not have autism.

Studies of genes linked to autism will help scientists determine how they might adjust future therapies for symptom severity. They have also found that genetic differences are not just "spelling mistakes" of codes making up gene DNA. They may also consist of repeated or deleted sequences and chromosome abnormalities.

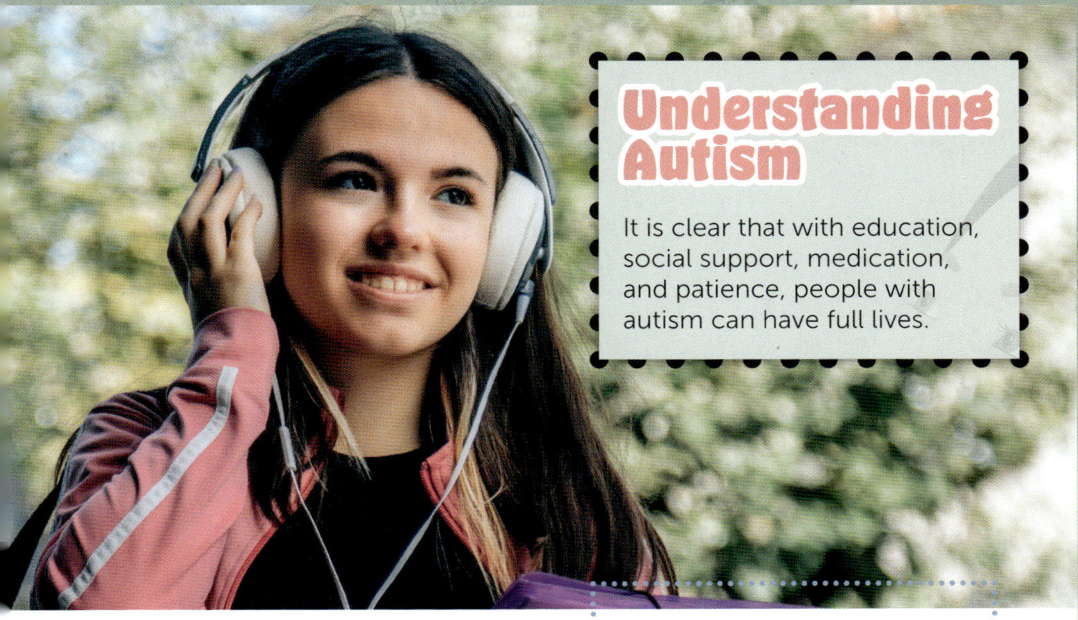

Understanding Autism

It is clear that with education, social support, medication, and patience, people with autism can have full lives.

Improved early screening will make sure children with autism are diagnosed quickly.

Thanks to collaboration with Google Cloud, the vast amount of information gathered about autism and genes is accessible to researchers everywhere at no cost.

"If we welcome neurodiversity in people, we can also welcome and appreciate all the positive aspects that neurodiversity brings. That makes for a more rounded, skilled society."

With improved education, medical help, and a more tolerant, inclusive society, the outlook for people with autism looks brighter than ever.

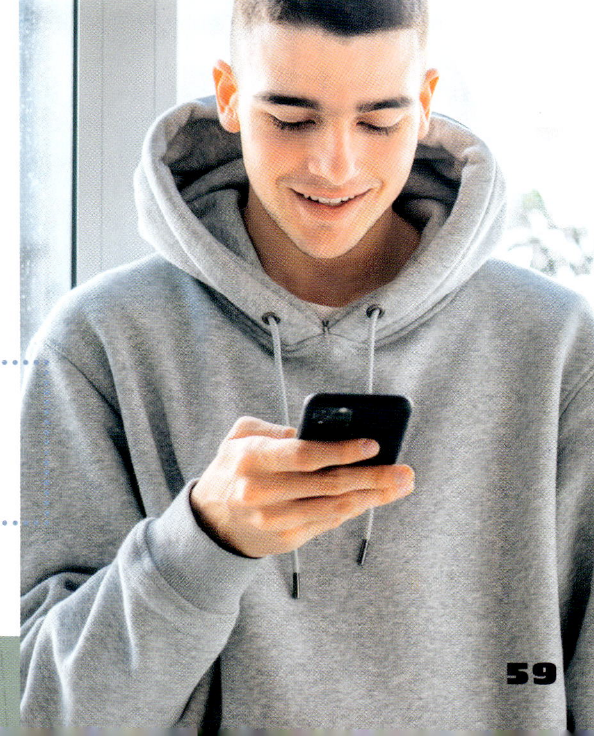

Glossary

antisocial not wanting to spend time with other people

anxiety a state of fear or worry

aromatherapy the use of essential oils for wellbeing

attention deficit hyperactivity disorder (ADHD) a disorder characterized by symptoms such as problems with focus and attention, extreme energy, and impulsive behavior

auditory related to hearing

bacteria tiny organisms that can cause infections or diseases

barriers things that prevent movement from one place to another

beneficial having a positive effect

bipolar disorder a mental health condition characterized by periods of extreme happiness followed by periods of depression

chromosomes threadlike structures found in cells that carry genetic information

contributions acts or things given that benefit others

coordination the synchronization of movements, mainly of the legs and arms

debilitating causing severe problems that make normal physical or emotional functioning difficult

definition a clear explanation

depression feelings of sadness and hopelessness

diagnose to identify the presence of a condition, illness, or disease

digestive related to the process of breaking down food, absorbing nutrients, and removing waste from the body

disability a physical or mental impairment that limits normal activities

diversity including a variety of people with different abilities, gender, beliefs, backgrounds, cultures, races, and experiences

DNA short for deoxyribonucleic acid. DNA contains instructions that an organism needs to develop, live, and reproduce

Down syndrome a genetic disorder characterized by intellectual disabilities, developmental delays, and distinctive physical features

empathetic able to understand and share feelings, thoughts, and experiences of others

fiber tough parts of food that help with digestion

genes tiny parts of every living thing that carry instructions for its development and function

gestures movements that are used to show thoughts or feelings

host cell a cell that provides a suitable environment for the survival of another organism

hyperactive having unusual amounts of energy

impacts has an influence or effect on something

impairment a physical or mental condition that limits a person's ability to do something

inclusive encouraging the inclusion of diverse groups of people

interact to communicate with something or someone else

interpret to understand the meaning of something

interventions actions to deal with a situation

inventive having the ability to create new ideas

involuntary done without thought

isolation feeling or being separated or disconnected from others, often resulting in loneliness

mannerisms physical movements that are typical of a person

modeling copying the behavior of something or someone else

modify to change something in order to improve it

motivates encourages

motor skills abilities related to the coordination of movements, such as walking, running, or picking up objects

mutations permanent changes in the DNA sequence of a gene

neurotypical refers to a brain that functions in the way it is usually expected to

nutritionists health professionals who advise people about food and healthy diets

obesity a medical condition characterized by having extreme excess body fat

obsessive continually thinking about something

overwhelming too much to deal with

predictable easy to estimate what will happen

psychological relating to mental processes, emotions, behaviors, or experiences

schizophrenia a severe mental disorder characterized by disturbing thoughts, emotions, and behavior

seizures sudden, abnormal electrical activity in the brain that can cause stiffness, twitching, or limpness in the body

self-esteem confidence in one's own worth or abilities

sensory related to the senses

sensory overload too much stimulation of the senses

sibling a brother or sister

stimulants things that trigger a response or reaction in a person

stimulate triggers a reaction

stimuli things that trigger the senses of sight, touch, taste, smell, hearing, and taste

subtle delicate and not easily noticed

symptoms the signs of illness

tolerant accepting and accommodating

umbilical cord a flexible cord that connects a fetus (unborn baby) to the placenta during pregnancy, supplying nutrients and oxygen and removing waste products

unbiased free from bias, or ideas that are unfair and are not based on fact

unique special, one of a kind

withdrawn avoiding social contact

Books

Grandin, Temple. *Different Kinds of Minds: A Guide to Your Brain*. Philomel Books, 2023.

O'Brien, Sarah. *So, I'm Autistic: An Introduction to Autism for Young Adults and Late Teens*. John Murray, 2024.

Purkis, Yenn and Tanya Masterman. *The Awesome Autistic Go-To Guide: A Practical Handbook for Autistic Teens and Tweens*. Jessica Kingsley Publishers, 2020.

Websites

For information on autism as well as support and events taking place, visit:
www.autismspeaks.org/what-autism

Find out more about autism and how you can help a friend with autism at:
https://kidshealth.org/en/teens/autism.html

Read articles on autism and find support at:
https://www.autism-unlimited.org/about/ what-is-autism/

Publisher's note to educators and parents:
All the websites featured above have been carefully reviewed to ensure that they are suitable for students. However, many websites change often, and we cannot guarantee that a site's future contents will continue to meet our high standards of educational value. Please be advised that students should be closely monitored whenever they access the Internet.

Index

About the Author

Sarah Eason has written many books for children and young adults. Researching and writing this book has highlighted the complexities of autism, from its causes to management, and the challenges that people with the condition face. She hopes this book is an informative, helpful, and compassionate resource for readers who are interested in the topic or affected by it.